That's Ju
The Way

That's Just
The Way I Am

Understanding
and dealing with
troublemakers,
wimps and oddballs

Willem van der Does

Cartoons by Peter van Straaten

CYAN

Marshall Cavendish
Editions

First published in Dutch as *Zo ben ik nu eenmaal!:*
Lastpakken, angsthazen en buitenbeentjes
by Scriptum Publishers, Schiedam, 2004

Translator: Jonathan Ellis

This translation first published in 2006 by:

Marshall Cavendish Limited
119 Wardour Street
London W1F 0UW
United Kingdom
T   +44 (0)20 7565 6000
F   +44 (0)20 7734 6221
E   sales@marshallcavendish.co.uk
Online bookstore www.marshallcavendish.co.uk

and

Cyan Communications Limited
119 Wardour Street
London W1F 0UW
United Kingdom
T   +44 (0)20 7565 6120
E   sales@cyanbooks.com
www.cyanbooks.com

A CIP record for this book is available from the British Library

ISBN-13   978-1-904879-59-6
ISBN-10   1-904879-59-4

Printed and bound in Great Britain by TJ International, Padstow, Cornwall

Contents

Foreword
Troublemakers, wimps and oddballs   **7**

Chapter
1   **Power and admiration**   **13**
Narcissistic personality

Chapter
2   **Attention and even more attention**   **41**
Histrionic (hysterical) personality

Chapter
3   **Egotism and ruthlessness**   **55**
Antisocial (psychopathic) personality

Chapter
4   **Instability and impulsiveness**   **67**
Borderline personality

Chapter
5   **Helplessness and submissiveness**   **79**
Dependent personality

Chapter
6   **Control and perfection**   **93**
Compulsive personality

Chapter
7   **Shame and fear of failure**   **109**
Evasive (avoidant) personality

Chapter
8   **Reclusiveness and reserve**   **125**
Odd (eccentric) personalities

Chapter
9   **Boundaries and possibilities**   **141**
Diagnoses, causes and treatment

Author's note   **157**

Foreword
Troublemakers, wimps and oddballs

Some people constantly get into difficulties, or cause difficulties to those around them, because of their character. These people may be suffering from one of the personality disorders recognized by clinical psychology and psychiatry. Only a few people actually have a personality disorder as such, but almost everybody has *elements* of this or that personality disorder. The characteristics are recognizable, at least if you know what you should be looking for. The cartoonist Peter van Straaten has a remarkably good nose for them. By looking at his drawings and reading my descriptions, you will learn to identify these characteristics and find out what it is like if they get out of hand and whether you can do anything about them.

What exactly is a personality disorder? People who suffer from one tend to get themselves into the same predicaments again and again in their work or study, in their friendships and in their intimate relationships. Sometimes their personality prevents them from ever enjoying such things, and they are left lonely and jobless. They are often unable to adjust their behaviour to changing circumstances, which makes other people think of them as compulsive and rigid. **1**

As a rule, people with personality disorders don't regard their behaviour as part of the problem. If you ask them why they keep doing certain things, they find it difficult to reply, or say "That's just the way I am."

A personality disorder generally goes hand in hand with serious suffering. It is not at all amusing; rather, it is tragic, irritating, pitiful or downright dangerous. However, the transitions from a "normal" character to an odd character and from an odd character to a pathological character are gradual. The milder forms can have amusing, entertaining or appealing qualities that make people cherish them or play up to them. **2** In such cases, what we have is not a disorder, but a personality style.

1

"NONSENSE. IT FITTED IN HERE
PERFECTLY YESTERDAY."

2

"I'M A DELIGHTFULLY CRAZY PERSON.
BUT YOU KNEW THAT, DIDN'T YOU?"

Most of the cartoons in this book illustrate not genuine pathology, but gentler everyday examples, and they are highly revealing. You can see these forms of behaviour in many people from time to time. After reading this book, you may even learn to appreciate your own idiosyncrasies a little better. **3**

By looking at the cartoons in context, the reader can learn to recognize personality pathology. The context I have used is that of the current psychiatric classification system, which recognizes ten different personality disorders divided into three groups: the dramatic, emotional types, the anxious, fearful types and the odd, eccentric types–*troublemakers, wimps and oddballs*.

Despite its psychiatric perspective, this book offers readers a feast of recognition. Not only does it bring the different personality styles and disorders to life, it also provides tips on how to handle them, and so is useful for anybody who has to deal with difficult or complicated people at work or at home. It should also interest readers who want to know how psychologists and psychiatrists see their clients, because it offers a peep backstage, as it were. Finally, it is suitable for students of psychology and medicine, for whom it can act as a complement to more traditional textbooks.

<u>3</u>

"SHE'S SO NATURAL, SO PURE, SO
GENUINE, SO PERFECT—I HATE HER."

Chapter 1 Power and admiration
Narcissistic personality

Characteristics

Vanity and conceit are the words most closely associated with the narcissistic personality. The term itself is derived from Greek myth. Narcissus was the son of a river god, and a youth of exceptional beauty. He fell so deeply in love with his reflection in the water of a stream that he could not tear himself away. He faded away through unrequited love, and in the place where he had sat, there sprang up a flower that took his name.

Modern narcissists are preoccupied with appearance, power and success. Their fantasy and desire is to be noticed and admired. **1**

A classic example of a successful specimen is a man immaculately turned out in a made-to-measure suit who has been able to manoeuvre himself into a position where he rules the roost and surrounds himself with yes-men. In textbooks about difficult people in organizations, the narcissist is frequently referred to as a tank or a bulldozer or some other similarly ominous epithet.

Narcissists try to be special and to make themselves stand out through what they consider to be their exceptional talent, or through their appearance and possessions. Only the most expensive gadgets, cars and holiday destinations are good enough for them. They need a great deal–a *very* great deal–of money, but if they manage to get it, they aren't too mean to spread it around, especially when others might notice. "Yes, it is a good suit. I had a tailor from Italy flown in specially. Cost a bob or two, but I can afford it, so why not? People are much too small-minded here. They look down on you if you have money and expect quality. In America, they respect you for it!"

1

"MY GOD—THAT MAN'S SO PLEASED WITH HIMSELF."

Narcissists make considerable demands on their partners' appearance, conduct and social status. In particular, it wouldn't do for a partner to have too many independent wishes or ideas that might conflict with the narcissist's own. **2**

What's more, partners are expected to feel happy–honoured, even–about their station in life: they are the chosen ones, after all. A partner who feels chronically unhappy is a blemish on a narcissist's reputation. **3** The odd incident of dissatisfaction or displeasure is acceptable, however, because it gives the narcissist the opportunity to step in and rectify things with some magnanimous gesture. For the classic narcissist, life is all about admiration and power; a partner is simply an instrument for obtaining these ends.

The packaging of a narcissist can, however, take on different forms that make him or her harder to spot. Narcissists who don't set store by their appearance can actually look exceptionally scruffy. They are arrogant enough to think that accepted dress codes don't apply to them, so you may find them wearing old jeans and a T-shirt at a gathering where everyone else is wearing a suit.

Occasionally, particularly in scientists, narcissism expresses itself as a determination to project oneself as intellectually superior. If a narcissist gets wind of an article or patent application in his field, he will elbow his way in and try and get his name on it. He thinks it only fair, since he has made an important contribution to the realization of the idea–although others may remember him saying he thought the idea stank. "So I did, but I was only playing Devil's advocate to help you sharpen up your thinking." Failing that, the narcissist will always remind you how much he has helped you in your career–and let you know that it's now payback time. Subordinates who have to submit their products to him for comment will get them back with his name written in above theirs.

2

"AND YOU'LL HAVE THE ASPARAGUS.
YOU LOVE ASPARAGUS."

<u>3</u>

"STOP THAT THIS INSTANT! THERE'S
NOTHING TO CRY ABOUT HERE."

Narcissists seem to feel that fortune has dealt them a very lucky hand. You'd imagine that people who consider themselves so wonderful might be resilient enough to withstand the occasional jolt. On the contrary, narcissists can't stand criticism. Their swagger is a form of compensation for deep-rooted doubt and a lack of self-esteem. Criticism opens up this painful wound, and the critic will have to pay for it. The vanity and conceit are fragile. **4**

Nevertheless, a degree of narcissism is healthy and promotes happiness and success in professional and social life. Narcissists are not slow to take charge, nor reluctant to throw their weight around. Narcissism can be a spur that helps people get into positions where they wield power. In addition, narcissists' conviction of their own superiority can rescue them from awkward situations and permit them to use tactics that most people wouldn't dream of using. The cartoon on page 17 features such a manoeuvre, undertaken, incidentally, by a narcissist who has been cornered, because admitting mistakes is not something he would do willingly. **5**

Excessive narcissism, on the other hand, can destroy happiness. Success is transient, and narcissists are extremely sensitive to criticism, sarcasm and any other signs that their power is waning. Innocent, well-meaning criticism is taken personally and viewed as a lack of loyalty. Narcissists who are in a strong position–the CEO of a large company, say–get rid of critics and independent thinkers or let them know their days are numbered. Other narcissists save themselves by changing their job, partner and circle of friends frequently. **6**

<u>4</u>

"OH REALLY? ALL MY OTHER
MARRIAGES WERE PERFECT."

5

"I ADMIT I'VE MADE SOME BIG MISTAKES. BUT BE
GRATEFUL—YOU CAN LEARN FROM THEM."

<u>**6**</u>

"NO, NO, MY FIFTH. JANE HERE IS MY FIFTH WIFE."

Narcissistic men can also become Casanovas, pursuing women compulsively whether or not they have a partner. Every successful seduction assuages, for a time, the ever-recurring fear of no longer being found attractive.

Narcissists expect perfection not just from their partner, but also from their children. They can't tolerate their children not getting everything right first time, or lacking talents and interests they consider important. Their children, like their partner, are a narcissistic extension of themselves. **7**

Narcissists believe that normal everyday rules and regulations don't apply to them. They think they should be excused if they clamber behind the wheel of their car when drunk, or if they aren't absolutely scrupulous about their expense account, or if they forget to register a share transaction, or if they take credit for other people's work. After all, "I have an important job, I work like crazy, and I've done a lot of good things."

Although there are aspects of such a life that might seem enviable at first sight, they conceal a restless and distrustful personality. This may be a comforting thought when you have to deal with an extreme narcissist in your own surroundings. Narcissists are addicted to adoration; the approval of others is the only thing that makes them feel good. They use other people as a mirror for gauging the scale of their own self-esteem. If others admire them, all is well–but not for long. Being somebody and being nobody are two sides of the same coin, and the coin can easily flip. Celebrity and anonymity are inextricably linked: celebrity can all too easily turn to anonymity. If adoration is withheld, or criticism voiced, the narcissist reacts furiously or suffers a sudden loss of self-confidence. If that happens, it's not easy to put things right again. **8**

7

"THAT'S JUST WHAT I WAS AFRAID OF.
THE iDiOT CAN'T FIND THE EGGS."

<u>8</u>

"OK, OK, OK – I TAKE iT ALL BACK. YOU'RE NOT A pRiCK."

Natural habitats

Successful narcissists are the most easy to recognize. You often find them in positions of status and power. Look for them in the top ranks of organisations, in politics and in the media. Indeed, some positions carry such severe disadvantages (such as loss of privacy) that only narcissistic people actively aspire to them.

The relationship works both ways: some positions actually nurture narcissism. Power corrupts; adoration corrupts absolutely. People who find that their talents put them in the spotlight (artists, top sports people, politicians, professors, leading doctors) run the risk that their narcissism is fanned to unpleasant proportions. **9**

But narcissism alone is seldom sufficient; most of these positions demand at least a modicum of talent. The less successful narcissists–those who are unable to obtain a glamorous position through lack of intelligence, social graces or luck– sometimes satisfy their ambition in voluntary organizations, staff associations or neighbourhood committees.

Extreme narcissists and those who lack talent will always come to a sorry end. You meet these bitter and cynical people almost everywhere. Some narcissists, though, can be extremely creative in thinking up ways of making themselves seem special. **10**

9

"GENTLEMEN, AS YOU ALL KNOW, I'M
JUST A COUNTRY BUMPKIN..."

10

"OH NO, NOT YOUR OPERATION AGAIN!"

Nemesis for narcissists

The younger specimens, those who are still making their way to the top, run a greater risk of coming into premature conflict with authority. Whether they have the staying power to ingratiate themselves with authority figures will depend on their intelligence and patience. If they lack patience, they will start their own company. A pitfall that a successful narcissist may fall into is that he begins to consider himself invulnerable.

He becomes increasingly high-handed in his treatment of subordinates, awards himself enormous pay rises, adopts a cavalier approach to expense accounts and claims credit for others' work. He barely even bothers to put in an appearance at the office, succumbing instead to the temptations of exciting extramural activities such as slap-up lunches with other narcissists. This leads to further erosion of his power base, though he may very well not notice. And because the top of most organizations is a vipers' nest, the narcissist is exposed to high levels of stress.

If the pattern persists, it is only a matter of time before he goes too far, and somebody objects. A trivial incident can trigger an all-out attack. Support evaporates, the narcissist is sidetracked, and his position becomes untenable. All that's left is a bitter man, incapable of understanding how this could have happened to him; it was such a futile incident, and after all he has done for everybody. . . The only thing left for a narcissist is to become a celebrity in his new role as victim.

Handling

An important characteristic of narcissists is their inability or unwillingness to take others into account. Although the first impressions they create may be positive ("He calls a spade a spade," "This guy can bring some life to a party"), those who know them better see them as cool, distant and calculating. In the end, everything revolves around them. **11**

Despite the egotistical core, the flamboyant packaging can exert an irresistible attraction on some people. Even those who should know better can be drawn in. Perhaps they recognize an appeal to their own megalomania ("I'll cut him down to size," "I know I can make him happy"), or they hope that the narcissist will admit them into the magic circle and allow them to bask in reflected glamour. **12**

Surprising though it may seem, the narcissist often manages to find forgiveness again and again. The outside world looks on in amazement at the way he uses his partner as a doormat while wrapping his flirtations and affairs in the cloak of love. Narcissists are able to focus intense attention on others for a limited time when they feel this is necessary to secure their continuing admiration. Partners are kept on a diet of "partial reinforcement": they frequently face rejection but occasionally hit the jackpot (imagine the narcissist as a one-armed bandit). **13**

What to do about the narcissist in your circle? The answer depends on precisely where the narcissist is to be found, whether he or she is permanent and unavoidable, and how the lines of authority run. Nevertheless, we can make a number of recommendations for possible treatment.

11

"I ASSUME YOU DON'T WANT TO TALK ABOUT IT?"

12

"I'VE HEARD A LOT OF BAD THINGS ABOUT YOU."

13

"DO YOU STILL CHEAT ON ME AS MUCH AS YOU DID, RUDY?"

Narcissists aren't inclined to see themselves or their behaviour as part of the problem: the fault always lies elsewhere. If you wish to adjust this perception, it is better to go along with the narcissist's vision initially before you introduce alternatives. If you want to get your narcissistic boss, colleague or subordinate to do something, flattery always helps. Make them amenable by regularly paying them a compliment or asking for their advice. If there is little reason to do so, make a weekly note in your diary: "Pay Jones a compliment."

If you think that a particular decision needs to be taken, go to your narcissistic manager and present her with the options in such a way that the decision becomes inevitable. Then give her all the credit for her vision and help in reaching the decision. You may have to swallow hard, but it will put you in good stead for the next time you have to get her to do something.

You may have to go a bit over the top to provide the right trigger for a narcissist: "Tom, I've selected you for this task because you are the only one with the necessary talent and perseverance. No, don't be so modest, it's a fact." But be careful; you can, of course, take things too far. **14**

Flattery doesn't mean that you have to approve of everything a narcissist does. On the contrary, that's a bad idea, since it will make them lose all respect for you. If they demand unreasonable things from you, you must put up resistance. Let's suppose that Mrs Wright doesn't feel like working overtime tonight. Clearly it wouldn't be wise for her to let her boss know that he is a self-centred egotist and that the parents' evening at school is far more important than those stupid promises he keeps on making to his customers. **15**

14

"IT WASN'T THAT FUNNY, MR. JOHNSON."

15

"MRS WRiGHT, I AM, I THiNK, JUST
TOO GOOD FOR THiS WORLD."

A much wiser course of action would be for Mrs Wright to agree that her boss is a paragon of virtue, and then take it a step further: how marvellous he is to keep the orders flowing in so that the company can thrive (or so that it can avoid filing for bankruptcy, given the terrible state of the market). But sometimes his goodness goes too far: customers take advantage and their demands become unreasonable and absurd. "I'm convinced the other board members would be grateful if you made a gesture –they simply don't dare do it themselves."

If all her flattery is to no avail, Mrs Wright will simply have to stand her ground and say it is absolutely impossible for her to work this evening. This could be tricky, because her boss is likely to fly into a rage at the first sign of resistance. If that doesn't do the trick, he may well start introducing irrelevant new arguments or call her loyalty into question.

Should something like this happen to you, try above all to keep yourself under control. Remind yourself that despite appearances to the contrary, this is not a personal matter–at least, not one that concerns you personally. If you allow yourself to get worked up, burst into tears, start shouting, give in or leave the room, it will certainly *become* a personal matter. The narcissist will put you down as an unstable or easily manipulated person, and that will be the start of a pattern.

Instead, stay calm, let him throw his tantrum, and repeat your message: it's impossible for you to stay late this evening. Even better, combine it with flattery: "Mr Bowman, I have considerable respect for you, but I simply can't stay late tonight." Carry on repeating it every time he introduces an irrelevant argument or insinuation. If he resorts to yelling at you, interrupt him by saying: "Mr Bowman, I hear you" and repeat your message. Stand firm even if you are quaking in your shoes. It can take a lot of energy and cause you a lot of stress, but follow these essentially simple rules and you have a chance of achieving the right result.

Be prepared for the narcissist's mood to swing in the opposite direction once you have stood up to him. Suddenly he notices you, asks your opinion or worse, even asks you out to lunch. **16**

Finally, when you are dealing with narcissists, don't make the mistake of thinking that their wisdom will grow with the years. The character traits of ageing narcissists become more pronounced, not less. This is because with the passing of the years their physical attractiveness wanes and the day approaches when they will have to make way to the next generation. The tricks they have to play to compensate for this nightmare and keep up their self-esteem become more and more extreme. **17**

16

"SAHIB! WHAT DOES THE WHOLE LOT COST?
I'LL TAKE IT OFF YOUR HANDS."

17

"DARLING, I'M MUCH TOO OLD FOR YOU."

Chapter
2 Attention and even more attention
Histrionic (hysterical) personality

Characteristics

The keywords for hysteria are attention, attention and attention. People with a histrionic or theatrical personality can't bear not to be the centre of attention. To stay in the spotlight, they will use any means at their disposal. The most common means is exaggeration, expressed not only through their appearance, but also through their behaviour. Their aim is to make an impression and get people concerned about them. To do this, they express and elicit all kinds of emotions as a compensation for their *idées fixes:* "I am unattractive" and "I can't possibly be happy unless others admire me."

A classic example is a woman who wears too much make-up and dresses in a style that is far too young for her age, creating a rather childish impression. She experiences strong emotions, but is easily bored and soon sets off in search of new thrills. **1**

Hysterical women dress provocatively and bask in the attention they receive. These are genuine *femmes fatales*: they flirt to attract a man, but react with astonishment and indignation if he actually wants to turn looks and words into deeds. **2** The suggestions created by their clothes, body language and behaviour never come to anything; the illusion is totally false. On the whole, women are better able to see through the impression than men.

The driving force of the hysterical personality is that it is crucial that almost everybody loves them for almost everything they do. This makes them hyper-sensitive to rejection. On the other hand, they can be as hard as nails, unable to form attachments and serially unfaithful. The thrill of the chase is so great that they can't stop themselves. Once they have trapped their prey, they lose all interest in him and set off in search of a new conquest.

<u>**1**</u>

"ISN'T iT TERRiBLy TiRiNG,
WALKiNG LiKE THAT ALL THE TiME?"

<u>2</u>

"WHAT'S THE MATTER? DO I SMELL?"

In addition to this flamboyant type of theatrical personality, there is also a more reserved, sphinx-like variety. These are people who attract attention by creating a veil of mystery. They dress conspicuously but in a rather old-fashioned style, and are anything but loud and expressive, preferring to sit quietly in a corner. Even so, they make sure that everybody has noticed them and sit with an astonished, mysterious, vague or slightly pained expression, staring straight ahead. Their demeanour suggests intense pain or profound aestheticism.

Although others may consider the emotions phoney, hysterical personalities experience them intensely and showily. They prefer to be led by their emotions. Their mental world is impressionistic and unarticulated, and they avoid deep intellectual discussions. To feel something is in itself sufficient justification for action. Hysterical personalities find dissatisfaction difficult to bear. If they are angry, they think they have the right to burst out in a rage; if they are happy, they are like children at Christmas. All of this can change from minute to minute, depending on the attention they are receiving.

You can be easily impressed by a moderate example, or if you meet one for the first time ("He's such a hearty, warm person" or "She certainly enjoys intense relationships"). You may even be jealous of them. When you get to know them better, they become tiring and you recognize the hysteria as something false, like a B-actress in a daily soap. Jealousy gives way to irritation and embarrassment. Some people realize this too late. **3**

Hysterical types will often fling their emotions into battle in order to get a response from the other person. If that doesn't work, they won't hesitate to ramp up their repertoire and resort to rage, fainting fits or childish whining. In fact, the emotional housekeeping of the hysterical type is immature: we all remember what childhood emotions were like. **4**

3

"YVONNE, I BEG YOU, PLEASE
DON'T ASK FOR THE RECIPE."

<u>4</u>

"BUT DARLING, JAMES DEAN
HAS BEEN DEAD FOR YEARS."

Hysterical types give in to their feelings without considering the consequences, which often makes them think in terms of black and white. She is a saint; he is a bastard. This is not an affectation; hysterical personalities actually experience life like this. Similarly, if the way they think about themselves suddenly changes, they can plummet into a deep pit. To others, it may look disproportionate and self-indulgent. But though the emotions may seem empty, it doesn't mean that the person involved doesn't suffer from them. **5**

Because the behaviour of people suffering from hysteria constantly changes, they can seem similar to some of the other personalities discussed here. They share their black-and-white thinking with the borderline personality and their desire for attention with the narcissist, and sometimes give the impression of dependency. People who enter psychiatry with this personality type may face a series of different diagnoses before the correct one is determined.

Natural habitats

The hysterical personality's habitat overlaps to some extent with that of the narcissistic personality. This is hardly surprising, since both hog the limelight and many narcissists have a theatrical bent. You may well spot them in professions that are in the public eye or have frequent media exposure, especially when the intellectual challenges of those professions are not too high.

Theatrical personality *disorders* are diagnosed more frequently in women than in men, which is somewhat unjust. In women, the behaviour (such as wearing revealing clothes) may be more pronounced, but highly macho behaviour in men can indicate hysteria. Hysteria is commonly combined with narcissism, and in men the narcissism tends to stand out more than the hysteria. And the apparently low frequency of hysterical personality in men also stems from the fact that people don't know what to look for. **6**

<u>5</u>

"IF IT'S TRUE THAT I BLOW EVERYTHING OUT OF PROPORTION, THEN ISN'T THAT TERRIBLE?"

6

"WHY DO I ALWAYS HAVE TO DEAL WITH
EVERYTHING ALL BY MYSELF?"

Handling

The first rule for handling a theatrical personality is to keep yourself under control. Don't let your expectations get too high. The behaviour of an hysterical person suggests depth–intense friendship, passionate love, uninhibited sex–but things seldom turn out that way. So don't be led astray by their wild and capricious emotions. Don't take too much pleasure in the admiration and affection that come your way, and don't get upset if your admirer suddenly ceases to notice that you exist.

Try to adopt an attitude of acceptance; hysterical people are seldom boring. Keep an eye on your limits. Your implicit message should be: no matter what antics you may perform, it's not going to make any difference to the way I behave towards you. Naturally, it is easier to maintain this attitude towards somebody in your circle of friends than towards your partner.

If they are to avoid being rejected by people who have grown weary of them, hysterical personalities would do well to seek each other out. Fortunately there is no lack of potential soul mates, as they would call them. Of course, they would have to be able to cope with all that competition for attention and stage-time. **7**

<u>7</u>

"STAY THERE, HENRY. I'VE GOT
THE MOST APPALLING COLD."

You may be able to achieve something with an hysterical personality if you try together to break through the impressionistic way of thinking. Think of an incident that was not too extreme and write down what the real problem was. Putting things on paper can be a good antidote to the theatrical personality's natural tendency to spring from one subject to another. Making lists can also help to adjust their exaggerated opinions about other people. If you are to achieve lasting results, you will have to tackle guiding thoughts such as "I must always be loved by everybody."

We live in an increasingly histrionic and narcissistic age, especially since the advent of 24/7 commercial television. Generations grow up with the empty emotions of daily soaps and the cheap instant solutions of dating and reunion programmes. No wonder so many people take them for the norm. **8**

8

"SHOULD WE MAKE UP ON TELEVISION,
LIKE EVERYBODY ELSE?"

Chapter
3 Egotism and ruthlessness
Antisocial (psychopathic) personality

Characteristics

The keywords for the antisocial personality are egotism and ruthlessness. These people are without a conscience. They have no regard for laws, norms or the rights and interests of others. "Hit them before they hit you" is their creed. They are dishonest and untrustworthy.

Antisocial personalities wind other people round their little fingers with tall stories, pretty promises and ugly lies. They are masters of seduction and know how to persuade others that their intentions are honourable. When they don't keep their promises (they seldom do), they conjure up yet another fiction to explain why. They leave others disillusioned, embittered and distraught.

Their deceptions are often calculated, but not always. Sometimes they come about because the antisocial personality realizes what the other person wants and makes impossible promises in an urge to reassure them or get something done. In general, antisocial personalities are impulsive. They are easily bored and hence drawn to exciting and risky activities such as extreme sports, fast driving, drug and alcohol abuse or provocative behaviour.

Extreme examples are not at all worried about committing the most appalling crimes, such as extortion, murder and rape. They have no regard for the consequences of their actions, and can't tolerate frustration. The worst cases are often to be found in maximum-security prisons.

Although they often have a superficial charm and can make a striking first impression, they are emotionally cold and think the whole world revolves around them. Their smooth presentation is all front, and maintained only as long as they think it is needed to get things done. Once they've got their hands on the loot, they reveal their true selves.

If an extreme narcissist can be compared to an emotional refrigerator, the antisocial personality is a freezer. Other people's interests matter not a jot as far as they are concerned; indeed, some take sadistic pleasure in others' discomfort. People who are too weak to defend themselves deserve, in their eyes, nothing better than to be taken for a ride. [1]

Antisocial personalities divide the world into two categories: people who try to take advantage of you and therefore deserve to be beaten, preferably before they beat you, and those who are weak and therefore deserve to be exploited. They feel themselves to be victims of an unjust society or a loveless childhood, and believe that gives them the right to take revenge. The fact that their victims have nothing to do with the imagined injustice is neither here nor there; if their victims had had the chance, they would have done much the same.

These tendencies are so extreme that it may seem that we are dealing with an illness, a deviation that you either have or don't have, with nothing in between. Not so: you come across milder forms of antisocial behaviour everywhere. The used-car dealer who sells a wreck to an unsuspecting buyer, the waiter who short-changes you, the executive who exploits every loophole he can find, the dole fraudster: they can all justify their actions by thinking: "If they're so stupid, they're asking for it." And that is a psychopathic style of reasoning. **2**

The impulsiveness and recklessness of antisocial personalities makes them seem fearless. Scientific research has shown that this is not just an impression: they actually do feel less fear than other people.

Another characteristic is lack of empathy: they are incapable of putting themselves in someone else's shoes. Seeing somebody crying or in pain, or suffering in some other way, causes a measurable reaction in people, but this reaction is much weaker in antisocial personalities. Yet this does not mean that they have no insight into other people's thoughts and emotions; in fact, many are highly skilled at pinpointing and exploiting another person's weaknesses. **3**

1

"THIS IS STILL A SERIOUS CRIME, SO IF I WERE
YOU I'D WIPE THAT SMILE OFF MY FACE."

<u>2</u>

"RULES, RULES, RULES. IT'S A SCANDAL.
THEY FORCE YOU TO RIP THEM OFF."

<u>**3**</u>

"ONLY JOKING!"

Psychopaths know no regret or shame, and are fairly indifferent to punishment. The threat of sanctions has no effect on their behaviour, apparently because of their low level of fear. Nor does suffering punishment lead to repentance. **4**

Quite the opposite: there is a danger it will only confirm them in their role as victim, which in turn makes them feel justified in seeking revenge.

Natural habitats

As we have seen, the more extreme examples of this personality type are vicious criminals serving long sentences in high-security institutions. About 80 percent of people suffering from an antisocial personality disorder have an addiction problem. Excessive alcohol and drug use can contribute to their impulsiveness. Many more men than women are diagnosed with this disorder. The worst cases are so antisocial and rude that they can never hold down a job for any length of time. But people with antisocial traits can be found in all levels of society. **5**

You have a good chance of spotting them in TV programmes such as *Watchdog*, which often feature exposés of confidence tricksters who leave a trail of unfortunate victims in their wake. When confronted by one of their victims or by a journalist asking for a comment, they react aggressively and deny everything, or turn on the charm: they are sorry for any trouble they have caused and are doing everything they can to put things right and pay back the money they owe. It is not difficult to guess how things will turn out.

4

"IF YOU CAN'T GET ME OFF, PERHAPS WE COULD
DO A DEAL. IT CAN'T COST ALL THAT MUCH, SURELY?"

<u>5</u>

"I HAVE TO LIVE HERE BECAUSE OF THE BLOODY TAXES."

Handling

In your personal life, you would be much better off not mixing with people with antisocial personalities. Unfortunately, they are unlikely to seek treatment on their own unless they are suffering from depression or other problems. The treatment readily available is not particularly effective; indeed, it can sometimes make matters worse. A programme of structured exercise, rigid discipline and direct confrontation can sometimes yield a degree of improvement. Any manipulative behaviour or denial of personal responsibility must be tackled immediately.

Living with an antisocial personality in your own environment is difficult. He will try to manipulate you with his charm and smooth talk, but turn his back on you when it suits him. **6** If you bump into somebody who seems excessively attentive and complimentary, beware. Distrust people who offer you the pot of gold at the end of the rainbow, and keep your greed in check because it will be used ruthlessly against you. Sometimes your distrust is initially allayed with geniality, generosity and gallantry. If you allow yourself to be impressed by promises made by people in flashy cars, don't forget to ask for a watertight guarantee before you give them any money. If the reaction is an indignant "But surely we trust each other," you'll know how the cookie crumbles. Finally, don't allow your own values to be distorted and try not to accept any favours. That will leave you in their debt–and it might be used to blackmail you. **7**

6

"TELL ME, DARLING, YOU DON'T HAPPEN
TO HAVE RICH PARENTS, DO YOU?"

<u>7</u>

"NO PROBLEM. YOU'VE STILL GOT ONE WHEEL
AND A LOCK. I'LL STEAL THE REST FOR YOU."

Chapter

4 Instability and impulsiveness
Borderline personality

Characteristics

The keyword for the borderline personality is crisis. People with a borderline personality are unstable and impulsive. They suffer from extreme and rapid mood swings that seem disproportionate to other people. They can start the day feeling fine, fall into a deep depression, and then flare up in a temper at some trivial remark. They can act on a whim and do things they later regret. In extreme cases, they take their anger out on themselves, and may cause themselves serious injury. Suicide threats and dangerous behaviour can also occur.

Although all personality disorders cause suffering, the extent of this suffering is most evident in borderliners, both for the people themselves and for those around them. Even so, borderline personalities–even those who have a personality *disorder*–are not always in crisis. There are intervals of relative calm.

People with a borderline personality have a variable image of themselves too: one minute they consider themselves worthless, the next they seem supremely self-confident. Their core thoughts are that the world is evil and dangerous, and they are vulnerable, powerless and inferior. Deep in their hearts, they consider themselves wicked and repulsive, but they crave acceptance and love. This internal conflict makes them latch on to other people and feel terrified at the prospect of losing them. Their tragedy is that they often act in such a way as to invite rejection. **1**

In addition, borderlines have a strong tendency to think in black-and-white terms, and nuances escape them. As a result, their relationships with other people are subject to enormous pendulum swings.

Borderliners often display a tendency to idolize those who make a good first impression on them. The object of their adoration may find this a strange but gratifying experience. "Wow! At last somebody realizes how wonderful I am." The trouble is, the attachment will end the minute you fail to live up to expectations. Sooner or later, you will tumble from your pedestal straight into the gutter. **2**

<u>1</u>

"I DON'T <u>DESERT</u> YOU EVERY MORNING,
I JUST GO OFF TO WORK."

2

"I'LL NEVER BE NICE TO YOU AGAIN,
BILL, JUST BEAR THAT IN MIND."

Once you have fallen, it isn't easy to redeem yourself. You have been consigned to the category of liars, cheats and bastards, and any attempt at reconciliation will be interpreted as a manipulative manoeuvre. Everything you say will be misconstrued and provoke furious outbursts. **3** And leaving things as they are won't help; it only fuels borderliners' rage. They won't let you get away with it; if necessary, they will threaten to kill themselves.

Anybody who has to cope with such an explosive personality would do well to make sure that their surroundings are relatively calm. Unfortunately, borderliners generate chaos and instability. They are easily bored and constantly on the lookout for new stimuli. If there is no conflict, chronic feelings of emptiness may get the upper hand. **4** Some experts think that the regulatory mechanism that controls emotions, functions differently in borderliners.

Since they also apply their black-and-white thinking to themselves, they are always restless, always searching for something. The image they have of themselves is not fully crystallized, or in flux. This may apply to their sexuality too. Borderliners are easily seduced by miracle cures that hold out the hope of helping them change their lives and attain peace, love and stability. **5**

As you might imagine, people with borderline person-alities find it hard to keep a regular job. However, you may encounter milder examples in the workplace. Look out for people who are constantly trying to form relationships with one or more co-workers while excluding others. Needless to say, the bonds don't last long, and new ones are constantly being formed, disrupting teamwork. Another source of disorder in the work-place is borderliners' habit of coming up with harebrained ideas and madcap schemes.

<u>**3**</u>

"SHOW OFF."

4

"EVERYTHING YOU DO, SAM, IS SO TERRIBLY UNCONTROVERSIAL."

<u>5</u>

"THERE WE GO AGAIN. TURNED TOTALLY
LESBIAN, AND YOU'RE <u>STILL</u> NOT HAPPY."

Natural habitats

People with a borderline *disorder* are much more likely than others to have been the victim of incest, violence or emotional neglect in their childhood. Their personal limits have frequently been ignored and trampled over. Sadly, they find it impossible even as adults to set their own limits, and they become terrified of intimacy. They may well have learned at an early age how dangerous it can be to trust people. Unlike the paranoid personality, who like them, distrusts other people, borderliners have no trust in themselves either, so they are forever searching for relationships.

Because of this, borderline personalities seldom enjoy lasting stable relationships, and they are highly susceptible to the guiles of swindlers and charlatans. There is a danger they will let themselves be exploited in an unhealthy relationship, or become disciples of some guru offering the promise of a better future. **6**

Borderline personalities can also be responsive to the saviour fantasies others may have. A relationship may arise in which they are the exploiter of a well-meaning but timid partner whom they intimidate with the threat of suicide.

Handling

Contact with somebody with a borderline personality is difficult and can be emotionally exhausting. Through their instability and volatility, they make constant demands on others and keep testing how far they can go. If you don't put a stop to this in time, you'll discover that you have no privacy left. The pressures of violent emotions, recriminations, depression and suicide threats send people off in all directions. Everyday events that are perfectly manageable for other people, such as changing an appointment, can induce such eruptive emotions in borderliners that they stand a very good chance of getting their own way. You simply can't keep up.

<u>6</u>

"WHY DON'T YOU TRY A NICE RELIGION FOR A BIT?"

The key to successful contact with a borderline personality is maintaining clear, consistent limits. You need to reach an agreement about the conditions for your relationship: we'll see each other so often, we won't do these things together, and I will react in this manner when you phone me to tell me how bad you are feeling. You will have to show that you consider the relationship worthwhile and that you couldn't care less how the other person behaves, even if they choose to stand on their head; you still think that they are of value and you won't be tempted to do things you've agreed not to do. The better you can keep this up, the greater the chance that extreme behaviour will die down.

There is a piece of comfort for borderliners and the people around them: many become mellower as they grow older, often around their fortieth birthday. **7**

<u>**7**</u>

"IF YOU THINK I'M DIFFICULT NOW, BELIEVE ME, I WAS
A LOT MORE TROUBLE WHEN I WAS HEALTHY."

Chapter
5 Helplessness and submissiveness
Dependent personality

Characteristics

Helplessness and submissiveness are the keywords of the dependent personality. Dependent personalities consider themselves weak, incompetent and incapable of sustaining an independent existence. They use all their strength to attach themselves to a strong partner whom they think will provide them with happiness and a buffer against the outside world. Unfortunately, they are in such a hurry to find a partner that they often latch on to the first person who shows any interest, which needless to say carries the risk of disappointment. **1**

First impressions can be very positive: dependent personalities may seem considerate, flexible and cooperative, and be good listeners. But their self-confidence is low, and they constantly seek approval and validation. This can, in turn, appeal to the other person's magnanimity. It isn't long, though, before their lack of determination and reluctance to voice an opinion begin to irritate. A dependent person is unlikely to undertake anything on their own initiative, but waits passively for signals from their surroundings about what is expected of them. **2** Their core idea is "I am weak and helpless." This gives rise to other ideas such as "If I'm left on my own, I'll be destroyed" and "Without somebody to care for me, I could never be happy." This gives rise to other ideas such as "If I'm left on my own, I'll be destroyed" and "Without somebody to care for me, I could never be happy."

Dependents' submissive behaviour can induce a variety of responses, often depending on how long you have had to deal with it. At first, things look promising: you are, after all, given all the freedom imaginable. So much freedom, in fact, that people can be tempted to see how far they can go. Sometimes it is very far indeed. **3**

<u>**1**</u>

"CAN I STILL SAY NO, OR HAVE WE PASSED THAT POINT?"

2

"TINA! I'VE FINISHED MY BOOK!"

<u>3</u>

"WE WERE SUPPOSED TO MEET HERE YESTERDAY."

The lady in this cartoon (page 83) has tried to dump her dependent friend, but has underestimated his sticking-power. Or perhaps she intended to force some kind of reaction; if so, she should be glad he actually admits that the date was for yesterday. The adhesive qualities of dependents can be infuriating and can encourage dominance in their partners. Sometimes dependence and dominance complement one another. In some cases, things can get so out of hand that a sadomasochistic relationship develops.

Dependents often appear helpless. They can function reasonably well with a strong personality at their side, but the thought of independence makes them panic. They seek out a strong personality who will manage their contacts with the outside world and make important decisions in life for them. For some partners, this can be an attractive role, appealing to the saviour in them, but it soon becomes confining and suffocating. Attempts to get the other to act more independently are doomed to failure, since dependents believe that independence equals loneliness. Ending a relationship with a dependent personality can also prove fraught with difficulty. The helplessness they exude can be so great that you may fear ending the relationship will cause a catastrophe. **4**

In common with the avoidant personality described on pages 109–123, dependents are anxious in their dealings with others, but this is mostly because of their craving to be cherished and protected. An avoidant personality avoids relationships out of a fear of criticism; a dependent personality clings to relationships. Dependents live in constant fear of being deserted and will do anything they can to gratify their partners' wishes. **5**

<u>4</u>

"AT THE TIME I THOUGHT HE WAS PATHETIC,
SO WE JUST GOT MARRIED."

<u>5</u>

"WHY DON'T YOU JUST ENJOY YOURSELF?"

Dependent people find it enormously difficult to take even the most trivial decisions without seeking approval or reassurance from someone else. Their automatic reaction is to go along with others or say they agree with them, even when they don't. Some people are so scared of disapproval or rejection that they never learn to stand up for their own opinions; indeed, they may barely possess the ability to develop them. They are sometimes "helped" in this respect by their partner's complementary character. **6**

Natural habitats

One thing dependents know for sure: they can't be on their own. You can often find extreme examples in relationships where they are dominated and even exploited. Such relationships don't always involve a partner; a dependent relationship can also exist with parents. For dependent personalities, the thought of being deserted is so terrifying that they sometimes allow themselves to be mistreated for years on end. The exploitation can assume considerable proportions: a dependent personality may tolerate years of physical abuse or turn a blind eye to a string of indiscreet affairs. More subtle forms of maltreatment can also occur, such as suppressing one's own needs and desires. **7**

If a relationship comes to an end, perhaps because the partner goes off with somebody else, the dependent personality will quickly find someone else who can provide the necessary care and support. Dependent people are susceptible to the seductions of charismatic figures, for instance leaders of sects, and also to political parties and action groups. Sometimes they develop a crush on their boss.

6

"JOHN, I NEVER CAN TELL WITH
YOU—MAY I LIKE THIS OR NOT?"

7

"QUITE SURE YOU'VE GOT EVERYTHING?"

Handling

Remember that the mere thought of independence and autonomy is terrifying for dependent personalities. Every attempt to change them will meet strong resistance if this central problem is ignored.

Any kind of change will have to be gradual; throwing somebody in at the deep end is pointless. Sometimes, their everyday skills and problem-solving ability have atrophied or never developed properly in the first place. Asking too much of them can lead only to fresh failures.

That's not to say that change is impossible. It is the dependents who are suffering most from their condition, so it is in their interests to change. It is usually advisable to avoid mentioning long-term aims, which seldom carry much appeal, and formulating general aims such as "becoming more independent" or "increasing autonomy," which can prove counter-productive. Much better to focus on small, concrete steps, such as "deciding where we will eat out together next time" or "stay away from my partner for at least half an hour at the next party."

It is important that dependents learn to think up such steps themselves. Their automatic inclination to allow their partner to dictate the conversation can be so deeply ingrained that this initiative is left to them too. **8** This is also a trap in psychotherapy: the therapist becomes the admired leader.

<u>8</u>

"LET ME DECIDE FOR YOU, OR YOU'RE
BOUND TO ORDER THE WRONG THING."

Chapter
6 Control and perfection
Compulsive personality

Characteristics

Control and perfection are the keywords of the compulsive personality. These people love neatness, order and predictability; they are also rigid.

Classic examples can be recognized by their meticulous appearance and spotless home. In contrast to the narcissist, who can also be carefully groomed, the compulsive is totally colourless. The narcissist is extrovert and flamboyant; the compulsive prefers to fade into the background. As with avoidant personalities (Chapter 7 *Shame and fear of failure*) compulsives' appearance can be mousy, with a wardrobe confined to a few variations on dull clothing. In much the same way, nothing is left to chance when furnishing the home. Chairs and sofas are arranged with mathematical precision, and nothing must be displaced. Books and CDs are regimented, as in a library. Everything has its place, and symmetry is all. **1**

Compulsives pay so much attention to detail that they lose sight of the whole. As a result, each individual aspect of a room may be perfect, but various aspects may clash with each other so that the final result looks tacky or messy. Moreover, compulsives find it difficult to throw things away, so things pile up; every newspaper supplement is carefully saved, resulting in enormous pillars of paper.

Meanness is another common trait. The compulsive is more aware of the uncertainty of the future than most people, and so has to set aside money for future disasters. House, kitchen and wardrobe are filled with bargains. Compulsives are also mean with their time: they have their own agenda, and if it is disrupted they find it difficult to adapt. A compulsive boss will try to make the most efficient use possible of their time, losing sight of the fact that work satisfaction and production would be much higher overall if they paid more attention to their employees.

Some compulsives lead an austere life. Their heating is always just a little bit too low; their lighting is dim. They always switch off the light when they leave a room, so that the rest of the household is always stumbling around in the dark looking for the light switch. Telephone conversations are brief, particularly if the compulsive is the one paying for the call. Even affluent compulsives think a cleaner is too expensive, or pay her such a pittance that she leaves in the shortest possible time, and so perfectionists can easily find themselves living in a mess. Some of them are miserly with just about everything. **2**

Taking a decision can be extremely difficult, because making a mistake is a cardinal sin for compulsives. If it is unclear what the right decision is, they can be paralyzed. They will take a long time to reach a decision, sometimes so long that it is no longer necessary. But once they have made their decision, it isn't easy to persuade them to change their mind. They are stubborn, and want to do things their way. If necessary, they will say "yes" and do "no." Spontaneity is not something you find in compulsives. They find it difficult to deal with ambiguity and uncertainty, and to recognize and talk about emotions. **3** The emotions they most easily acknowledge are disappointment, remorse and fear. If things go wrong, they can easily become sombre or depressed.

Their core fear is that they will no longer be able to stay on top of things and will get snowed under. To avert and compensate for this, they develop a system of rules. If they want to achieve something, they try to gain complete control over their own behaviour and that of everybody else involved. They are strict regulators, so they make others feel pressurized and coerced. Often, though, they get bogged down in detail, so their aim is never achieved or achieved only after considerable delay. They sometimes get stuck in preparations, and never get round to the real work. **4**

<u>**1**</u>

"WHY ARE WE IN SUCH A MESS?"

2

"OH HEAVENS, ARE WE ECONOMIZING
ON THE THYME AS WELL?"

<u>**3**</u>

"SINCE I'VE BEEN WITH YOU, I HAVEN'T LAUGHED ONCE."

<u>4</u>

"OR SHOULD I JUST FORGET ABOUT MY
DOCTORATE? WHAT DO YOU THINK, ANNE?"

People with a compulsive personality have unrealistically high standards both for themselves and everyone else. This can be deeply frustrating for the people around them, not only because compulsives make impossible demands, but also because they have rigid ideas about exactly how a particular goal should be reached. **5**

Compulsives are excessively dedicated to their work, at the expense of relaxation and friendships. They always want to be doing something useful. If they go on holiday, they take their perfectionism with them, which can mean that their travelling companions don't experience the trip as the holiday that was intended. **6**

Having a compulsive personality is not the same as having a compulsive disorder. The latter, often called obsessive–compulsive disorder, expresses itself as a fear of contagion or an urge to control. People who are diagnosed with this disorder spend hours of every day performing a range of rituals such as cleaning their house, washing their hands or checking their locks. This is a stubborn and crippling disorder that can take over their whole lives, but it can be treated with medication or behavioural therapy. However, people with a compulsive personality don't have a mild form of the disorder, and they run no greater risk of developing it than other people do.

5

"... BUT MAKE SURE THE SAUCE IS LIGHT
AND FLUFFY, WITH JUST THE BAREST HINT
OF TARRAGON, AND GO STEADY WITH THE
BALSAMIC VINEGAR..."

6

"HOW MANY ROMAN CHURCHES
HAVE WE STILL GOT TO DO, PHILIP?"

Natural habitats

Unless they have a sadomasochistic streak, compulsives don't like working in teams. They get much too irritated by the way their colleagues work, and *vice versa*. Delegating is also anathema to them, because not delegating saves them a lot of uncertainty and monitoring. The perfectionism and dedication that milder examples show in their work can be advantageous. Indeed, in some professions (air-traffic controller, surgeon, accountant), somebody who is slightly compulsive can be rather reassuring.

Working with a compulsive personality can sometimes make life easier for those around them: since there is only one way for a compulsive person to do a job–*their* way–they will take a big chunk of the work out of your hands. **7** The disadvantage is that this can lead to delays and prove counterproductive, with the whole thing getting bogged down in detail. **8**

What's more, compulsives have the unpleasant habit of making their colleagues feel they are slacking, sloppy and thoughtless in their work. Should everybody agree that it might be a good idea to deviate from the rules just this once, you can expect a sermon about the importance of rules, their history, how dangerous it can be to take those first steps along the slippery slope, and so on and so on.

This behaviour is, needless to say, not confined to work; family and friends are also put to the test. Compulsives can be seen as people with an exaggerated conscience and as rigid. **9**

Handling

Extremely compulsive people can have a paralyzing effect on productivity, not only for themselves, but also for the people they have to work with. It can help to give them a relatively isolated position in the organization. If it works, everybody is better off, and colleagues won't be tempted to resort to more extreme measures. **10**

<u>7</u>

"I'VE GOT TO LEAVE A BIT EARLY,
SO I'LL DO THE REST AT HOME."

<u>8</u>

"WOULD YOU LIKE TO BRING THINGS TO A CLOSE?"

<u>**9**</u>

"I KNOW YOU MEAN WELL, RICHARD,
BUT I'M SO FED UP WITH YOU."

10

"I'LL NEVER CATCH HIM MAKING A MISTAKE.
CAN'T YOU JUST PESTER HIM INTO LEAVING?"

The tragedy of this unproductive behaviour is that it is motivated by the need to do good and help people. This is one of the reasons why compulsives find it so hard to make decisions: they may disappoint someone. Things can sometimes be speeded up if somebody helps the compulsive through the decision-making process. They should ascertain exactly what is causing the delay. Is the compulsive concerned about the reaction of someone in particular? Discuss how to deal with any possible negative reactions, but emphasize that this person isn't made of porcelain and can withstand a jolt or two. Promise the compulsive that you will support them after the decision has taken effect, and keep your promise. It can also help to list all the pros and cons and weigh each one, and thus approach the decision process systematically. Include in your calculations the disadvantages of delaying the decision.

Such strategies can also be helpful when explaining a decision to a compulsive. If you are inclined to take decisions intuitively, perhaps by visualizing your decisions or following your gut instinct, you will have to understand that this approach is incomprehensible to a compulsive. You may need to spend extra time and energy to convince them, but the results can be rewarding.

If you have to deal with decision-avoiding compulsives in your work, you may be tempted to avoid consulting them. This is understandable, but seldom sensible. The saving in time that you achieve will probably be wiped out by the extra time you will spend when the compulsive discovers they have been ignored. In the long term, it may pay to ask more for advice, particularly in cases where only one decision is really possible. Imagine you are authorized to make decisions about purchasing, and you are reviewing a number of quotations. If one of them is clearly the best, consult your compulsive manager about your proposed purchase. He or she will quickly agree with you, giving both of you a feeling of satisfaction. What's more, your manager will start to develop a conviction that you are the right kind of person: "Jones really sticks to the rules." You can use this later to your advantage.

Chapter

7 Shame and fear of failure
Evasive (avoidant) personality

Characteristics

Shame and fear of failure are the keywords of the evasive personality. People with this personality type are extremely shy and scared about what others may think of them. They believe that they are incompetent and worth less than other people, and they fear being rejected and making a fool of themselves. So terrified are they of failure that they behave awkwardly and may make others think they are odd. The things they fear most– blushing, being at a loss for words, looking nervous–are more likely to happen to them than to other people. **1**

That, however, is not the core of the problem. Evasive personalities are so focused on themselves that they become hypersensitive. If they feel the slightest bit warm, they may imagine their face is on fire, even though nobody else has noticed a thing. They also have strange ideas about what others will think of them. They will immediately assume not only that other people have seen their blush, but that they will consider it bizarre and aberrant. The possibility that someone else might consider blushing perfectly normal or even charming doesn't occur to them. Worse still, they assume that other people will think not "She seems a bit nervous today" but "What a bundle of nerves! What an awful person!"

And so they become trapped in a vicious circle in which they conjure up ever more unpleasant illusions about social contacts, and invent elaborate excuses to avoid them. They can't go to a birthday party because of prior commitments or a sudden bout of flu. They don't dare embark on a relationship unless they can be sure in advance that they will be accepted and liked. Some evasives rarely venture outside a small circle of family and friends.

Being noticed is a constant fear. People with this personality dress as inconspicuously as possible, sit like wallflowers at parties and think they have nothing of interest to say to anyone. So self-effacing and insipid are they that a lot of people ignore them altogether. **2** They seek cover and avoid eye contact, so you have to overcome an obstacle simply to talk to them. If you persevere, you will probably receive so little response that you will assume the conversation is embarrassing them, and give up. People sometimes misinterpret evasives' behaviour as lack of interest, and find it irritating. **3**

In contrast to schizoid personalities (page 133), who also avoid contact as much as possible, evasive personalities actually yearn to participate in social life. They would love to have friends, be intimate with others and voice their opinions, but the fear of being hurt or rejected prevents them taking the first step. An evasiveness that may have begun in their childhood often means they lack the most elementary social skills. They often have fantasies in which everything turns out fine for them in the end, but these fantasies tend to involve some kind of magical intervention because they haven't the faintest idea how to achieve this for themselves. **4**

A further complication is that people with this kind of personality frequently feel frightened and gloomy, yet find themselves unable to tolerate these emotions. Instead of taking action, they try to avoid their feelings by cutting out social contact, or suppress them with alcohol or sedatives.

The core fear for the evasive personality is that they will make a fool of themselves. "If people get to know me better, they'll see what I'm really like, and drop me like a ton of bricks. I couldn't bear that." The cartoon on page 116 shows how an evasive man's nightmare has become reality. **5**

1

"OH, THAT'S MY BOYFRIEND. HE'S A BIT SHY."

2

"DON'T WORRY, SHE'S ENJOYING HERSELF."

3

"OH LOOK, THERE'S GEMMA WITH
HER WALKING LAMPPOST."

4

"WHY DO WE KNOW SO FEW INTERESTING PEOPLE?"

5

"YOU'RE A SWEET, VULNERABLE MAN, DICK,
BUT WE'VE SEEN SO MANY SWEET, VULNERABLE MEN
THESE PAST FEW YEARS THAT THEY'RE COMING
OUT OF OUR EARS."

Natural habitats

Evasive personalities prefer to stay at home, but they aren't very happy there because they feel they're missing things. Cancelling an engagement may bring a brief moment of relief, but recriminations quickly follow, along with self-pity about leading such a restricted existence. Evasives often work below their true intellectual level because they look for a job where they can work largely alone, without having to take part in too many meetings. They tend to hold positions where they have little contact with other people. In the lunch break, they often have work that must be done to keep them away from the canteen. Company parties and receptions are avoided with a battery of excuses. Evasives attend meetings in silence, keeping any criticism they may have to themselves, or mentioning it later in the mildest possible wording. **6**

They daren't go into a relationship unless they are certain they will be accepted. Once a relationship is established, they will go to any lengths–even sacrificing their own interests–to keep their partner happy. The occasional healthy conflict is not something they understand. Some partners find this an attractive proposition; they can do as they like and not worry about the consequences. If they do come in for any criticism, it's usually too late to make any difference. **7**

One disadvantage is that your partner will stick to you like glue at parties and other social events. Some people find the evasive's unresponsiveness and lack of drive infuriating. **8**

Handling

The sensible thing to do depends on the seriousness of the problem, but in general it doesn't help to throw an evasive personality in at the deep end. Failure is virtually assured, adding to the inferiority complex. The first step the evasive personality must take is to exchange his or her daydreams about how wonderful things could be for short-and medium-term goals that are actually attainable. That means working with small, clear steps expressed in specific and concrete terms: not "relate normally to colleagues," for instance, but "have lunch in the canteen at least once a week, and put up with the anguish it will cause me."

<u>6</u>

"YOU KNOW WHAT I FIND A TINY BIT AWKWARD?
THAT WE'RE ONLY TOLD THINGS <u>AFTER</u>
THEY'VE HAPPENED."

<u>**7**</u>

"THAT ROMANTIC WEEKEND IN PARIS
THREE YEARS AGO—WHY DID WE NEVER GO?"

<u>8</u>

"YOU MIGHT AT LEAST <u>TRY</u> TO
HAVE A DECENT ARGUMENT!"

It is no use trying to put everything right in one go. It may even be necessary to start by developing social skills: how do you continue a conversation when you notice you are stammering? What can you say at a party other than "How do you know the host?" If you can help dispel the strange ideas the evasive personality has about other people, so much the better. Can he really be sure that other people notice him blushing? Even if they do, does it necessarily mean they'll write him off as a wimp? What's so dreadful about a few people not liking you? The tragedy is that all this evasion doesn't help the evasive person; in fact, it often makes things worse. If other people notice how they try to hide, they may feel irritated, start giving gratuitous advice or avoid the evasive person altogether. **9**

Taking the first steps towards normal social relations is especially difficult when you know it will be accompanied by tension and fear–feelings that evasives have such difficulty in dealing with. Sometimes they think they are the only person who has such feelings. It can be comforting to be told that everybody shares their experiences. About 50 percent of people find it difficult to speak in public. Even more are scared of examinations, job interviews and personnel assessments.

There is one more thing that can help evasives take that first step: the realization that even if you do nothing at all, people will still pass judgement on you. In any case, whether you do anything or not, your influence over what others think of you is limited at best. **10**

9

"YOU REALLY SHOULD TRY TO SAY SOMETHING AT THE NEXT MEETING, MR. GOODWIN, EVEN IF IT'S ONLY A JOKE."

10

"NOBODY HATES ME."

Chapter
8 Reclusiveness and reserve
Odd (eccentric) personalities

The eccentric category consists of three disorders that in some way or another resemble schizophrenia. Schizophrenia is an extremely serious disease that can easily become chronic. There are indications that the disorders that belong in the eccentric category are genetically linked with schizophrenia. People with these disorders may have inherited a less severe form of the disease, so that they exhibit fewer and milder symptoms.

Schizophrenia can influence all psychological functions: observation, thought, speech, will and feeling. Symptoms include delusions of persecution (for instance, the belief that one is being bugged by secret services), hallucinations (hearing voices, seeing visions), confused thought, confused speech, and a lack of willpower and energy (staying in bed for hours on end). Not all patients show all these symptoms. The symptoms come in episodes (called "psychoses") that usually last for a few months, but can be over in a single day or persist for years, and tend to be accompanied by extreme anxiety. Patients can tolerate very little stress and run the risk of becoming socially isolated. Medication can reduce or eliminate the symptoms and improve resistance to stress.

The three personality types that fall into this category seem to represent three different aspects of schizophrenia. People with a paranoid personality suffer mainly from suspicion, and have difficulty trusting people. The schizoid personality seems cold and reserved, and has little need for human contact (the reclusive type). The schizotypal personality exhibits the more bizarre symptoms of schizophrenia, but in a milder form: people behave oddly, see things in a strange way and have peculiar thoughts (the eccentric).

The cause of these three personalities should be sought in genetics. There are strong indications that the schizotypal personality disorder is connected to schizophrenia; for the other two, research results provide conflicting evidence.

Paranoid personality

Characteristics

Suspicion is the core characteristic of the paranoid personality. Patients with paranoid schizophrenia are firmly convinced that there is a conspiracy against them, whereas people with a paranoid *personality* have less grandiose ideas about the threat they are under. They are seldom psychotic, which means they have not lost their grip on reality. Nevertheless, their ideas are so extreme that they obstruct normal contact with other people.

Paranoid personalities are unfailingly suspicious and mistrustful. They doubt the loyalty of their acquaintances and colleagues and see threats in every mundane event and remark. They assume that other people's motives are dubious and find all sorts of evidence to prove it, ignoring anything that demonstrates the contrary. Their central ideas are "Other people act out of malice and can't be trusted" and "Give the other person a chance and they'll bite your hand off." They expect to be deceived, exploited and put down, and are always on their guard.

Unfortunately, they find plenty of evidence to support their convictions. To be sure, people don't always act out of good intentions, and human behaviour is complex and open to interpretation. A paranoid person is often extremely reserved, yet prone to making insinuations about others. **1**

Close friendships are difficult to achieve; paranoid personalities never see any fault in their own behaviour and automatically lay the blame on others. They have a short fuse, and are quick to go on the offensive. Forgiving and forgetting don't come easily to them, and after a trivial incident they can harbour a grudge for years. **2**

Paranoid personalities who have a partner will be domineering and restrictive, sometimes even tyrannical. They operate strict house rules and won't think twice about enforcing them, through intimidation if necessary. Sometimes they have an elaborate security system in their home, which betrays the fact that their driving force is fear. Deep inside is a very scared individual. The partner of a paranoid personality may find it

127

<u>1</u>

"THAT'S GREAT. GO ON, SAY SOMETHING
ELSE THAT'S HURTFUL."

2

"BUT THAT WAS IN 1958 YOU'RE
NOT STILL ANNOYED ABOUT IT?"

very difficult to end the relationship. A paranoid man may keep a grip on his partner for years by saying that she is just as worthless as everyone else, and she will leave him in the end, and then his life will not be worth living. Sometimes fear of physical violence will prevent a partner from packing her bags and leaving.

Paranoid personalities easily relapse into stereotypical thinking; for instance, they may lay the blame for their (or the world's) problems at the feet of Jews, foreigners, trade unions, government or big business. In milder forms, this "externalization" can be common; it has the advantage of relieving you of your responsibility for difficulty or failure. **3** The drawback, of course, is that you don't learn from your negative experiences, and that you will have to find new whipping-boys and scapegoats time and again.

Natural habitats
You find paranoid personalities shut up in their houses writing letters to the ombudsman or appeals tribunal and building up hefty dossiers. Occasionally, you may catch a glimpse of one in TV programmes like *Judge Judy* with some improbable story about a neighbour from hell. They may also appear in programmes that try to track down missing relatives, such as the parent who suddenly disappeared and is still not inclined twenty years later to talk about what went wrong.

Handling
Clearly, dealing with a paranoid personality is not a stroll in the park. Much better to do without them in your working environment; they poison the atmosphere and spend most of their time casting aspersions. On the other hand, they can sometimes inspire you with ways to get out of your responsibilities. **4**

In your personal life too, you'd be a lot better off without them. Unfortunately, they aren't inclined to undergo treatment. After all, there's nothing wrong with them; other people are the problem. Another reason may be that they hate psychologists.

3

"WHAT ON EARTH DO YOU SEE IN THAT THEO?
HE WASN'T EVEN BORN HERE."

<u>4</u>

"DO YOU BY ANY CHANCE HAVE A
CONSPIRACY THEORY WE COULD USE?"

All in all, it is extremely difficult to deal with a paranoid personality. It is often difficult to avoid feeling offended by their distrust. Sometimes their accusations hit a weak spot, and give you a nasty feeling of guilt. Attempts to convince them you are trustworthy may very well rouse their suspicions and thus prove counterproductive. It is better if you accept their distrust and gradually prove your trustworthiness through your behaviour. That doesn't mean you should accede to unreasonable demands, though. Just tell your husband you are having lunch with a friend, even if he has suspicions about "that woman." If you have to watch every word in case you let out where you have really been, the end is nigh. One thing you should avoid, though, is the use of humour or banter. A paranoid personality can't cope with it, and rectifying the damage you do could take years.

Schizoid personality

Characteristics

The schizoid personality is reserved and lacklustre. There may be a superficial resemblance to autism, but without the language disorders that characterize this condition. (There are no indications that autism and schizoid disorder are genetically related.)

Schizoid personalities are hermits, neither desiring nor enjoying relationships with other people. To others, they seem cool, distant and emotionally lifeless. Their social skills are not well developed and they seem immune to criticism or praise. They simply do as they please, preferably on their own. They are loners who do jobs that require little social contact. **5**

These people are happiest when they are alone. They often realize they are different to other people and sometimes, perhaps urged on by concerned relatives, attempt to be more sociable. But their attempts are doomed to failure: they simply don't know how to start a conversation and keep it going, and worse still, they don't really care. **6** Sometimes they find an ally with whom they build up some sort of social contact, maybe drinking beer together in silence while they watch football on TV. If one of them happens to move away, even after years of companionship, the contact will simply cease.

<u>5</u>

"DO YOU ACTUALLY HAVE A <u>SOUL</u>, ANTHONY?"

<u>6</u>

"... AND HE READS QUITE A BIT ..."

<u>**7**</u>

"HIS EVEN TEMPER DRIVES ME MAD."

Natural habitats

Schizoid personalities prefer to stay at home. The kind of job they like features a lot of computers and few people. Colleagues who try to make contact with them–maybe because they are irritated by this silent piece of furniture in the background, or because they worry about their loneliness–meet a brick wall. **7**

Handling

Since schizoid personalities feel no need for social contact, there's not a lot one can say about handling them. Pestering them doesn't help in the least. On the contrary, it will provoke yet more evasion and force them further into their shells. Resist the temptation to try to prod the schizoid personality into action through extreme statements or behaviour; it will probably achieve the exact opposite. **8**

You might do best by letting them do their own thing and showing them respect. If you want to build up some kind of connection with them, allow plenty of time and take things gradually. You may just gain a better insight into the world of the schizoid, and succeed in helping him or her take small steps into a broader social network. But don't expect too much.

Schizotypal personality

Characteristics

Peculiar ways of thinking are the central characteristic of people with this personality type. Others see them as reclusive or eccentric. Their appearance and behaviour appear odd; they often wear strange combinations of clothes, for instance. **9** What's more, their speech can be vague and long-winded, but without becoming confused, as may happen with schizophrenia. They have strange ideas and apply odd reasoning, and can be profoundly superstitious or have problems with magical thinking (the belief that thinking a thought can make it turn into reality). The emotional life of schizotypal people is also odd; they show few emotions, or display inappropriate emotions such as laughing at something tragic. Their ability to concentrate is limited.

<u>8</u>

"THE WAY YOU'RE NEVER JEALOUS—THAT'S JUST SICK."

<u>9</u>

"OH, THAT'S HARRY. I KNOW HIM FROM WAY BACK. HE'S STILL SEARCHING FOR HIS TRUE IDENTITY."

Natural habitats

These people mostly go their own way. Social situations scare them. Because of their eccentric behaviour, long-windedness and inability to concentrate, they have an even smaller chance than the schizoid personality of holding down a normal job. Sometimes, though, less acute examples find a way of earning an income by exploiting their supposed gift. They offer their services as clairvoyant, healer or some other paranormal guru. That's not to say that everybody who claims to have paranormal gifts is schizotypal, but it may certainly help. TV programmes about strange people regularly feature people with schizotypal personality traits.

Handling

Since schizotypal people become terrified by anything but the most superficial contact, possibilities to enjoy contact with them are extremely limited. Here again, your best bet is to let the person do their own thing and show them respect. You don't have to pretend that you believe what they believe, nor that you can even imagine what they experience. Simply say that you don't share their experience. Trying to convince them they are wrong or seeking to get them under control is not a good idea. It will increase the distance between you, or cause a great deal of stress. This can in turn worsen their ideas and make them lose contact with reality (psychosis).

Chapter
9 Boundaries and possibilities
Diagnoses, causes and treatment

Diagnoses

Do you recognize yourself in any of the personalities described here? Well, I do. In fact, I recognize in myself aspects of disorders from all three categories. Does that worry me? Of course not— that's just the way I am . . .

If you too see yourself in this book, do you have cause to worry? Probably not; personality disorders are not particularly common. There is a chance that reading this book has given you student's disease: the inclination to recognize all sorts of symptoms in yourself, and to draw the conclusion that there's something wrong with you. **1**

Perhaps you recognize somebody else in one of the types I have described? Be careful, and don't jump to conclusions. There are a number of psychological mechanisms that make you quick to judge that someone else has a pathological character.

First, there is attribution bias. Attribution bias means that when something unpleasant happens, people apply different norms to themselves than they do to other people. If a nasty thing happens to you, your immediate reaction is to think the fault lies elsewhere: someone else has behaved badly, or you are suffering from bad luck. If you see something unpleasant happen to somebody else, your perspective is different: it's all the fault of the victim, not the surroundings.

Take those shares that you bought a few months back with your hard-earned savings. Now they are worth only 70 percent of what you paid for them. No doubt you'll think you've had unbelievable bad luck to have bought just before the economy stagnated, or else lay the blame on those incompetent financial advisers. If the shares belonged to anyone else, though, you'd be more inclined to think they shouldn't have been so stupid as to buy them.

1

"NO, THERE'S NOTHING WRONG WITH YOU.
YOU'RE JUST TERRIBLY UNHAPPY, THAT'S ALL."

A second mechanism that can lead to your drawing the wrong conclusions is confirmation bias. This happens when you have limited information about a person's character and you use this information to draw more or less automatic conclusions about other aspects of their character. The result is what is called "implicit personality theories"; some may be correct, but others are way off track. If somebody laughs a lot, he must be a nice guy, or happy; somebody who is highly intelligent will probably be arrogant. What's more, you may start behaving in line with your implicit personality theories. Without realizing it, you may provoke behaviour in other people that confirms your ideas.

In some cases, we form an implicit personality theory about somebody even though we have no information about them other than hearsay or the way they look. **2**

Was it a good idea, then, to publish this book? By placing all these recognizable cartoons in a particular context, I may have created yet more implicit personality theories, and made you think all sorts of normal behaviour are pathological. That accusation is not completely groundless, hence this warning. On the other hand, we all have a number of implicit personality theories; it's unavoidable. But diagnosing actual personality disorders is difficult, and this book is no substitute for a careful examination by a clinical psychologist or psychiatrist.

I have tried in each of my descriptions of the different personality types to build up a sketch; I have not tried to itemize the precise criteria as they are defined in the official diagnostic system. A list of criteria has limited use, since deciding whether any particular criterion is present calls for training and experience. What's more, the criteria themselves may change whenever there is a new edition of the classification system, since research into the personality continues. But if you like, you can easily find the criteria for every personality type on the internet, along with all sorts of tests you can take to help you diagnose whether you have a personality disorder. Be careful, though; these tests invariably overestimate the number of people suffering from disorders. Many healthy people are misled into thinking that they have a disorder, or even several different ones.

2

"YOU HAVE TO WATCH THAT BOY;
HIS GRANDFATHER WAS A BROWNSHIRT..."

Even clinical psychologists and psychiatrists are seldom able to make a reliable diagnosis after a single consultation, and will refuse to do so. All sorts of psychiatric symptoms that may well be temporary or can be treated, such as depression and panic attacks, can make it impossible to reach a personality diagnosis early on. If somebody is depressed, he or she is more sensitive to rejection and may appear to have an evasive personality; treat the depression and the evasive traits may disappear. Asking patients how they felt before depression struck doesn't help because people suffering from depression have a highly negative view of the past.

Finally, some people are just unlucky, and through no fault of their own live in terrible circumstances. Having a lot of problems in life is not the same as having a deviant personality.

Causes

Libraries are filled with tomes on the causes of personality disorder; even so, there are few solid facts. Broadly speaking, three factors determine your character: genetics, shared envir-onmental influences (the aspects of the environment that you have in common with your siblings, such as style of parenting) and unique environmental influences. Theories about personality disorder have in the main concentrated on environmental aspects, but recently the influence of genetics has become clearer. **3**

<u>3</u>

"YOU'RE NOT GOING TO BE A BASTARD
LIKE YOUR FATHER, ARE YOU?"

For normal characteristics, such as whether you are introvert or extrovert, the genetic influence, as established from research with twins, is estimated at 50 percent. The remaining 50 percent is almost completely attributable to unique environmental influences; shared environmental influences appear to be much less important. This does not mean, however, that genetics automatically account for 50 percent in the determination of personality disorders. It is still possible that the development of extreme variants–personality disorders–is determined to a higher degree by the influence of environmental factors on genetically determined temperaments. For some personality disorders, such as antisocial and schizotypal, it seems certain that the genetic component is considerable. On the other hand, an adopted child who grows up in a criminal family has an increased chance of developing an antisocial personality, so genetics is far from being the whole story.

Research into the causes of personality disorders is proving extremely difficult. It is virtually impossible to base any conclusions on individual life histories. If somebody with a theatrical personality tells miserable stories about emotional neglect during their childhood, for instance, it may seem obvious that this neglect is the cause of the disorder. **4**

However, parents who neglect their children are likely to have some pathological traces in their personalities. Not only are their children exposed to neglect, but they may also have inherited genetic material from their parents.

In addition, clear differences in children's temperaments emerge at a young age, making it possible that different children within the same family might induce different parental styles. In these cases, differences in parental styles seem to cause the difference in personalities. In reality, however it is down to a combination of nature and nurture.

Sometimes parents do such terrible things or are so inept and oafish that it is hard to imagine that their children will not bear the scars. But having scars is not the same as suffering a psychiatric disorder or a disturbed personality.

<u>4</u>

"THAT'S LOVELY. WHY DON'T YOU DO ANOTHER ONE?"

Therapists have used extensive clinical experience to develop theories about the cause of some personality disorders. For instance, if a child has to make huge efforts to get their parents' attention and finds throwing tantrums is the only way to do it, extreme emotions can become an end in themselves, and even a justification for their existence. Such neglect could play a role in hysteria, or in the whole category of troublemakers. In the category of wimps, it seems plausible that a lack of love and an excess of criticism or control play an important role. **5**

What's more, it may well be that the example parents give their children also plays a role, and that children copy their parents' behaviour.

But as we have seen, research into causes is complicated. During therapy, you can ask hysterics about their life history, but it is difficult to tell whether the subjective experience they have of their youth has been coloured by their current pathology. If someone says that they didn't get much attention from their parents, you have virtually no way of knowing whether this is objectively true. **6** And we shouldn't lose sight of the fact that therapists base their theories on the people who come to their practice. Since they don't see people with similar childhood experiences who lack a personality disorder, their view on the importance of upbringing may be biased.

Treatment

For quite some time, people with actual or suspected personality disorders were not particularly popular with psychotherapists. The therapies available brought little relief, and patients would regularly suffer crises. But then, a few decades ago, psychotherapy in general brought little relief. **7**

5

"WE ARE VERY DISAPPOINTED IN YOU, JOSEPH."

<u>6</u>

"YOU'RE NEARLY EIGHTY. YOU CAN'T GO ON
BLAMING YOUR PARENTS FOR EVERYTHING."

7

"YOU SHOULDN'T EXPECT TOO
MUCH FROM THIS THERAPY."

People with personality problems who were fairly robust were eligible for psychoanalysis: an hour on the couch every day for years on end, talking about anything that crosses your mind. All your personality problems are played out in your relationship with your therapist, so providing a vehicle for change. Classical psychoanalysis is now definitely in decline: the theories on which it is based are wrong, it requires an enormous expenditure of time, money and effort, and the results are downright disappointing.

Much has changed since then. More effective methods of treatment have been developed for depression, anxiety and other conditions from which many people with personality disorders suffer. These treatments involve both psychotherapy and medication. People with personality disorders may also profit from such treatments, although the treatment may take longer. For some personality disorders, building up a relationship of trust can take a considerable time.

In recent years, more and more treatments aimed specifically at personality disorders have been developed and tested. The goal of such treatments has become much more realistic. In the old days, if treatment was available, its aim was sometimes a complete rebuilding of the personality; nowadays, the aim can be defined as changing a personality disorder into a personality style. This is not the same as "you'll just have to learn to live with it." Aims are defined in accordance with the nature and severity of the problem and the stage of the treatment, such as learning to prevent and manage crises, improving social skills, learning to regulate emotions and changing basic thought patterns.

The nature of the therapy is different to that of psycho-analysis. Instead of consciously creating and working through a dependency relationship, therapists now do as much as possible in cooperation with patients. Sessions are much more structured, and often draw on exercises, role play and homework assignments. Even in these treatments, though, the relationship between patient and therapist can sometimes become strained. The model may be a cooperative one, but the patient is still in a dependent position. That can induce conflict and stir up emotions, and it can be therapeutic to work through them together. Of course, everything depends on the nature and severity of the problem.

As we have seen, treating personality problems is not easy; it demands patience and often takes a lot of time. If the problem is serious, the treatment can last for years, though not necessarily on a weekly basis. One final piece of advice: if you contact a therapist and he or she suggests that you take a seat on the couch five days a week for an indefinite length of time, just turn and run. **8**

<u>8</u>

"I THINK A LITTLE THERAPY—SAY SIX OR SEVEN
YEARS—SHOULD CLEAR THINGS UP IN YOUR HEAD."

Author's note

The classification system that informs my text is the *Diagnostic and Statistical Manual of Mental Disorders*, fourth edition (DSM-IV), published by the American Psychiatric Association (Washington DC, 1994). When writing this book, I consulted a number of abnormal psychology textbooks, namely those by S. Nolen-Hoeksema (McGraw-Hill, 2001), G. C. Davison and J. M. Neale (Wiley, 2001), and J. S. Nevid, S. A. Rathuis and B. Greene (Prentice Hall, 2003). In addition, I made use of my own clinical training and experience and the books I read in that context. The most important are *Cognitive Therapy of Personality Disorders* by A. T. Beck, A. Freman & Associates (Guilford, 1990), *Practical Management of Personality Disorders* by W. J. Lively (Guilford, 2003), and *Handbook of Diagnosis and Treatment of DSM-IV-TR Personality Disorders* by L. Sperry (Brunner-Routledge, 2003). Finally, I have been inspired by popular psychological books such as *Coping with Difficult People* by R. M. Bramson (Dell Publishing, 1981).

Peter van Straaten has been publishing a daily cartoon in several Dutch newspapers for many years now. His unusual talent for depicting human personalities is exemplified by the fact that all I had to do was select from his vast body of work; I had so much choice that we didn't have to commission a single cartoon for this book.

My wife, Ineke Booij, is a psychiatrist and extraordinarily perceptive in recognizing personality types. She has assisted me enormously with the writing of this book. I would like to thank Tosca Ruijs of Scriptum Publishers for thinking up the wonderful cover. Robin van Emden read the manuscript and made useful suggestions. Naturally, I accept full responsibility for the ideas and possible mistakes in the text.